PLATO'S BREATH

May Swenson
Poetry Award Series

PLATO'S BREATH

poems
by

Randall R. Freisinger

UTAH STATE UNIVERSITY PRESS
Logan, Utah

Utah State University Press
Logan, Utah

Typography by WolfPack

00   99   98   3   2   1

Library of Congress Cataloging-in-Publication Data

Freisinger, Randall R., 1942–
Plato's breath : poems / by Randall Freisinger.
    p.   cm. — (May Swenson Poetry Award series)
ISBN 0-87421-228-6
I. Title. II. Series.
PS3556.R3939P58   1997
811'.54—dc21   97-4727   CIP

for Joseph, for Linda,

&

for what remains
available

CONTENTS

Although Randall Freisinger excels at rendering the familiar, workaday world of an American Midwestern childhood and young manhood—family dinners, shop class, baseball games piped in by radio, sexual fumblings in the backseat of an Oldsmobile—the poems of *Plato's Breath* don't settle for thumbing through memory's photo album. From the opening poem, "Saved," Freisinger conducts an inquiry into "the fledging of souls." Violence, fear, and death stalk through his poems as palpable presences and mysteries to be deciphered: a girl "born without a face" who resembles a Picasso portrait, his father's aphasia.

Driven by a rigorous mind, *Plato's Breath* unflinchingly tests the "pestilential waters" of racism and ignorance. This quest to "glimpse what waited on the other side/ of need" yields the benedictions of small, incremental enlightenments, states of grace. It is rare these days to find in American poetry any interest in metaphysics. But in *Plato's Breath*, even the Kirby man, a vacuum cleaner salesman, wrangles with big questions, though Freisinger's under no illusion that he can "trap the immensities of the moment" or infinity. Despite his humbling bafflements, though, he persists in his anatomies.

Readers will find both ear and mind pleasurably roused by the music of Freisinger's meditative poems—"Hints for Dissection: *Gray's Anatomy*," "Plato's Breath," "On a Child's Nose Swallowed by a Dog," for example—which abjure the flat, minimalist sentences and fragments so much in vogue these days. He weaves instead long, looping skeins of thought, like verbal counterpoint, that close on a note of exultation, as in "Antediluvian: Kansas City, Summer, 1953":

> Even then his life was a knot
>
> > badly tied and slipping, that first moment
> > of an improvised solo when melody,
> > swiftly pared to its lowest common terms,

gets lost, as surely as memory is lost,
scattered by wind, earth, flood, jumbled
gravel of rivers, found again like bone and clay
riddles we glean from earth with soiled hands
that we might understand abandoned meanings.

I believe May Swenson would have enjoyed Randall Freisinger's *gravitas* lightened by self-irony, his savoring of droll words like "*schnozzle, nozzle, bugle, beezer, / beak*, and his curiosity about the dark, misshapen underside of human behavior that's partially redeemed by blessings "struck at random in this catacombed night!"

Plato's Breath brings welcome news of a mature talent.

Herbert Leibowitz

ONE

SAVED

When I was a boy with a mind
soft and Baptist as potter's clay
I played in an alley a few blocks
away, hanging out, watching
the presses at Steele Cleaners hiss
out great steam angels
into the dimming afternoon.
One day bells from the nearby Convent
began to toll with such urgent pealing
I knew the world must be at its end
there and then beneath an odd lemon
tint of apocalyptic sky.

          I ran
nowhere and everywhere at first,
then homeward, certain I would find
burning Seraphs lining Tracy Street,
Jesus, blood still streaming
from His pierced hands and feet,
calling my neighbors and parents
from their evening papers and warm
plates of dinner, herding them out
to the pavement into quaking
huddles of saved and damned.

The corner turned on anxious Keds,
I saw Jeannie Satchel in her yard at practice
with her baton, at thirteen already famous
all across the city for her twirling routine.
Billy Wakefield was punting long and
perfect spirals up and down the street.
Mrs. Archer was mowing her lawn
for the third time that week. My father
hailed me from the front porch swing

where he swayed, his day's edges smoothed
by stiffer and stiffer drinks. Mother was at her stove,
the odor of frying meat a gall and flay
to my agitated state. Upstairs, my brother
the sinner was playing Elvis in the bathroom
mirror, combing his rebel's hair, coaching
his lips toward their permanent sneer,
his hips twitching to the uninhibited beat
of *Jail House Rock,* their demons still
not yet cast out.

              I descended
into the basement's semi-dark,
still half expecting Gabriel's knock
or promised trumpet calling us home.
On my work bench were spread
paper plans, my Flying Tiger,
its delicate balsa wings pinned
and left to dry. I sat, twisted off
the cap from my tube of Duco Cement,
sniffed, lifted like Icarus into sun-
beckoning sky. I opened my heart
to Jesus in mumbled prayer, not quite
certain if it was gratitude or fear,
then fumbled for the string that hung
from the bulb overhead, found it,
paused with the infinite patience
of the saved before I pulled, hard.
Let there be light, I said.
There was, and I set to work.

Someone had to cut the timber, plane
and fashion it into its simple design.
          Someone had to leave home with a belly

full of breakfast, kissing his wife and kids
at the door, nails heavy in his carpenter's pouch,
          his hammer dangling at his side, a sign

of honest trade. While the flies went about
their commerce in the mid-day heat, someone
          had to be deaf enough to such terrified screaming

to drive those nails through feet dusty and palms
pale, perhaps mis-striking, failing as anyone might
          to hit squarely the nail's head, coming down

hard on instep or thumb. Someone
had to help raise up the splayed weight
          of heretics and thieves that they might hang

there for a time, public and shamed. And someone
had to see the likeness in that hill. Was it
          the mounting count of sun-bleached grins,

a simple fact, then, of denotation? Or did someone—
a servant, perhaps, looking up
          from her half scrubbed floor, or a whore

waking after a night of normal business—
did someone, staring from great enough distance,
          note sameness between the thrust-up earth's

curves and the elemental shape of our
boney pan for brains that contains all
          we desire and what we're willing to pay?

AFTER READING WORDSWORTH'S
PRELUDE, BOOK I

> *. . . And I grew up*
> *fostered alike by beauty and by fear. . .*

School-less summer days I shot sleeping
frogs with my BB gun
or searched the vet's trash
for dead cats and dogs,
poked at glazed gelatinous eyes
with sharp sticks, inflicted cold
exploratory kicks, being half struck
dumb by the terrible loll of tongue.
The patient bloats of fur
stirred my own muzzled fears
with the distant puling of pups.
The rising stench of animal piss
spurred the whirl and gossip
of congregational flies.

Next door, the cool transactions of
the Blue Hills Poultry House.
There, men in black
rubber boots and gloves
shoved wing-flapping fury
head first down tin cones mounted
to a slowly spinning wheel.
I remember mill-red combs, white
throats exposed, eyes spitting
rage at the hand-held knife
as the drum spun cleanly
through the blade's fixed grin.
Bodies stiffened, toes scuttled
on tin while men hosed away
sluiced blood.

Plucked down
rose like unfledged souls,
then sifted back to the brick
floor like benedictions. I followed
the newly dressed to roosts
of ice where they rested beneath
headstones of pound and price,
amazing to naifs like me, ignorant
of the phoenix: flames, ashes,
and resurrection.

Out the door I stepped and crossed
the street to the Texaco station,
young, innocent, whistling,
as if I had just placed Christ
on my tongue and now could slug
him down with a bottle of grape
Nehi, salvation's bloodless cup.

ANTEDILUVIAN: KANSAS CITY, SUMMER, 1953

Tonight the lamp burns archival
as I read of Charlie Parker's Kansas City
days, antediluvian nights of buck twenty-five
bop at the High Hat, El Capitano, Aladdin
Hotel, nights of cheap hustles, hocked
horns, dope, dirty tenement rooms and needles,
nights along The Paseo, wild, amniotic
cats from joints on Vine Street, jazzed and jamming

in parks, passing pints of Sweet Lucy
wine, Bird wearing his sorrows like a hip suit
of clothes. Those sweltry nights of '53
when he was back from New York or Paris to
rage at Tutty's Mayfair, Blue Hills Gardens,
I prayed, hot and penitential, thanking Jesus
for America, my white skin, for setting me
down clean and well-fed, not a "pickaninny"

in crumbling "Niggertown," a place
of no concern, Father promised, a distant
place of pestilential waters held back by dikes
dividing the city. Such nights I listened
to the baseball Blues, Larry Ray's play-by play,
naive to how from studios only miles away
he made me believe he was in a booth
on the road in Toledo, Omaha, Indianapolis.

Soon I was lullabied to sleep by libidinous
whispers of maples while downstairs my parents
drank Coke and Seagrams, tuned Bing,
the Dorseys, Benny Goodman, Perry Como
and Vaughan Monroe on the Philco. My parents,
fleeing from nothing, fearing nothing but thoughts
of flinching within reach of The American Dream.

What I knew of blackness? Little more
than "nigger," a word, its referent dreaded
but remote as comic book words like "Jap,"
"Kraut," "commie," the slit-throat it conjured
blurred by "junglebunny," "sambo," "jigaboo,"
"coon," pictures of Uncle Remus, Aunt Jemima,
radio guises of Rochester, Amos 'N' Andy.
These things too I knew: the jeweled field of light
at Twenty-second and Brooklyn, black boys

quick as water striders in stadium traffic,
waving red bandannas, hawking spots
in dust-caked yards to park. I knew
Vic Power's arrogant preening at first,
Elston Howard crouching like a shadow
behind his barred catcher's mask.
These were the minors, Yankee dreamers,
and I was eleven, apprenticed to fool's

gold dreams of the majors, an age
another boy spent leaning against walls
in alleys behind clubs, listening
through brick to Lester Young,
fingering notes and chord changes
to get them right on his imaginary horn,
patient in his passion, a young Apollo
waiting. Even then his life was a knot

badly tied and slipping, that first moment
of an improvised solo when melody,
swiftly pared to its lowest common terms,
gets lost, as surely as memory is lost,
scattered by wind, earth, flood, jumbled
gravel of rivers, found again like bone and clay
riddles we glean from earth with soiled hands
that we might understand abandoned meanings.

Perhaps it was the heady scent of pine
and paint and turpentine, perfume
to a boy in seventh grade. Fractions and divisions
were too abstract, even when shrouded in words
about how fast Bill could run if he was one third faster
than Phil. In shop, problems were made real
by rumors of boys past who had subtracted
index or pinkie from hapless hands, heedless boys
who shirked school's principal rule of thumb:
Pay attention! For half of our last year, we mastered
the basic tools: ruler, jigsaw, chisel, file, drill,
hammer, glue, clamp, and sandpaper. We crafted
and stained gifts for Christmas and Mother's Day:
ashtrays, bookends with horse heads in profile,
lamps in layered ovals or made to resemble
little covered wells, the rope's handle hooked
to the socket's chain. Pacified by the steady whine
of machines and the zone coverage of Mrs. Burroughs,
our tall, raw-boned teacher with twin linebacker brothers
playing for the Oklahoma Sooners, we were happy,
and for that hour thought hardly at all
of girls, who were up in Home Ec learning
the economies of cakes and balancing acts of teacups
on plaid-skirted knees, or how to chat with ease
about life's beveled nothings. Three floors beneath
such domestic scenes, we rudely pounded away
at our stubborn metals and woods with awkward
unsymmetrical grace, tooling, schooling ourselves
in the metaphysics of mistakes we soon enough
would make, learning how to hide or, tight lipped,
accept a clumsy fit, a mismeasured distance.

THIRTY-FIFTH BOMBING MISSION, CERIGNOLA, ITALY

for Richard Hugo

When the man comes saying time
to fly, you know the implacable
drawl five miles up through flak,
your bombsight screwed
to children cadging shadows
in a place without borders
near Odertol.

        At the Red Cross
in Foggia, coffee's shrove,
Goodman, Dorsey, Bunny Berrigan's
trumpet solos. You think of the empty
field near Spinazzola where the war went
slack and you surrendered
to wind that urge to murder
and create.

        When only hours
later on the skirts of Canosa a woman
begged cigarettes, in spite
of the field you denied her.
How easily we slip
into this ungenerous world
of denial and possession: this
you brood years later
at the factory, wading streams
for browns, drinking whiskey
at hotel bars.

        Near forty
you return to find that field
of wind farther from town
than you remembered, surprised

you came so far once
only to speed by it
now in a car with nothing
to say, no thought of stopping,
leaving it behind,

        the way we turn
wordless from an open grave
when silence is our sole
remaining lien on the dead.

STOPPING TO DANCE
for Jim Goetz

Twenty-five years since I failed you
in Freshman English, becoming one
good reason for you to leave that small
Missouri town and make your mark
on this black marble wall filling
its space like a scream. Now I look
you up on lists thick as big city
directories, as if the years had brought
enough change and a chance to explain
from such long distance.

                    I search
along this chain of flowers, amulets,
gifts, the chiseled litany of names
until I find yours, point it out
to my wife and sons, touch it
for proof of my right to one little
piece of the grief that surrounds us,
as if to say I too have been changed
forever by chemistries of the war
I evaded: privileged, white as paper
campaigns I waged, armed with college
degrees and teacher deferments.

                     I see
you in class, bent to your books,
a handsome boy all tense and twisted
by Eleusinian mysteries of syntax and usage,
of ruled spaces where nothing ever cohered.
Your essays came to me fingerprinted,
grease from your '57 Chevy, themes
about football games against House Springs
and Crystal City, about how you wavered
looking that first time down barrel-blue

steel at a deer, tales about illicit beers
and wars of fists behind Opel's Cafe or
The Magic Carpet.

                In-country only
weeks, you came back like a gift,
flag-wrapped, boxed, a lone Marine your sole
companion. In time-lapsed footage, I saw
your girlfriend turn, peach-cheeked queen
to local barfly, drinking too much,
fucking every farm boy with a pickup
truck and half an acre
to his name.

              Valéry said
to understand one another we must pass
quickly over words, which bridge
their chasm only if we do not rest
to look down, to think about them, straining
language with the dead weights
of our bodies. Only poems dare
to stop, he said, caring to understand nothing,
deferring sense whenever they please
just for the aimless pleasures of dance.

CATALOG PEOPLE

Against all the old and well-meant warnings
they've slept with it unresolved again,
more so by their willed and failed attempts
at making love. Themes of loss needled sleep,
and they've stumbled downstairs before light
footfalls of their children. Waiting there,
the emptiness of nothing to retract.
Coffee. Implacable jack-in-the-box
of toast. Kids, their senses wrapped
like periscopes round blind corners
of breakfast dishes. Either could break
this distance but that the tally says
it's hers to turn.

         At the counter,
a pot of coffee in her hand, she lingers
before catalogs from yesterday's mail,
blanching at the lean, tan, athletic figures
more handsome and explicit in their freeze-
frame bliss than Keats's urned lovers,
more poignant and young in pure silks and
cotton twills, more brilliant in
hues of peach and jade and raspberry,
pinstripes, polos, docksider shoes.

Her hunger billows with unexpected breeze:
I want us to be like these people,
the ones in the catalogs, she blurts.
He stumbles in a sudden surf of something
not quite pain, but it serves, like
the *Yes* he summons, the gesture
of his cup as he reaches for her
robe's sleeve to pull them both again
safely back from the dark side of words.

FIRST FANTASY

Other than Mother, the one
I am not supposed to remember,
she was nameless, slightly older, her lips
and hips and face all moon-shaped and filled
with gravity new to my weightless state.
Some days she would simply appear, alone,
from the fringe of a small woods
behind the field where my team practiced.
From my spot at shortstop or on deck,
ready for my turn to hit, I'd watch
her delay her return to that woods,
her breasts leavened beneath her simple
blouse and of sudden interest, her eyes
aimed (or so it seemed) purely at me.

Were it not for the watchful eye of the coach
I might have dropped my glove or Louisville Slugger
right there in the hot July dust and gone
to that inarticulate place with her,
this pitiless goddess each boy follows
to an elfin grot at least once.
At home, locked in my room, I could shut
my eyes, let my hands roam while the locusts
yearned outside my window like a Wagner chorus.

Now I am the coach, the one in charge,
and sullen young girls pass the summer
trolling the road that runs past our practice field.
So far when my players chase fouls
across that road, they have all returned,
sometimes bearing gifts of turtles
or frogs from the water-filled ditch.
The others cluster around, but I see
how one or two allow their eyes

to drift to where this or that girl stands,
waiting, flashing the signs my hands
have no power to wipe away.

SPRING BURIAL

The body dies; the body's beauty lives.
—Wallace Stevens,
"Peter Quince at the Clavier"

When the local disappeared fishing
off Portage Entry on Father's Day last June
already you'd heard the first morphemes
of pain begin to whisper
their one simple sentence, like the abstract
sound of sense we hear in halls
from voices behind doors that muffle
the words.

A hundred yards out
from where you grilled steaks,
boats and divers grappled the deadpan
lake while you tried to tell your sons
the meaning of *drowned.*

Never early with deadlines,
you made a plumb line of dying
the next month and took not Christ
but Bentham on your tongue
while the other—still missing,
presumed drowned—arabesqued unseen
between present and past participles.

Now when it's May, time for Spring
burials, and the dead who've lain
bunked in windowless brick all winter
have returned to the town's streets
on flat-bed trucks to burgeon
and bumble with lilac, apple,
and bees, news comes

of another reprise: on a distant
beach in Canada, ice and wind-

pestled shreds of clothes, keys,
bones, a surgical screw.
The body is believed . . . etc., say the papers
and speak of positive identifications.

Dear friend, if something in this ended dance
appeases, we plead the heart's split
measure, the way the dead's last breath
gives breath back to the living, the way
passion to move our own bodies through
space feeds on finished movements
like this coda to your *pas de deux.*

for Bruce Petersen

In the booklite's beam, *Gray's Anatomy*, inscribed by the woman
who gave it to me. Whose snapshot suddenly slips now from
    between pages,
a photo I've carefully misplaced of a moment at Walden Pond,
one of those last-day-together tableaus unfinished lovers
hide exactly where they know they will find it years later,
just in time to mar the finish on a life they've barely managed
to bring to a tolerable sheen.

Her face, caught in a moment of rare repose, how it contradicts
the book's placid, exact engravings, its matter-of-fact language, prose
so clipped to suit the clinical scene I can almost see Gray's students,
full of theories and memorized lists, gathered in class around the
    cutting table, ready
at last for the sobering praxis that grounds a healer's art.

Still heavy with last night's wine and lust and blood,
perhaps they have just come from the dizzy carousel of a lover's body,
needing to be reminded once more that beneath the chill
casing of this cadaver's leathered skin they must now begin in earnest
learning how to suspend their faith in meanings,
how to accept the body as patient architecture: *jamb, cartouche, quoin,
cheneaux.* The soul, whatever it might once have been,
jury-rigged and Janus-faced, having vanished into boundless space
like light from a burnt-out basement bulb.

I see them learning their ancient tools: saw, hammer, scalpel,
small barbless hooks and string for lifting and holding
in hard-to-reach places, wood blocks for tensing muscles too much
    at ease
in the comfortable shoes of death. What else needed
but a geometer's sense of spaces and a deeply rooted desire to expose?

I stare again at this face that once touched me so deeply,
trying to recall her body, to imagine it thus open and revealed,
as if the secrets I failed ever to approach might—had my hands
only possessed the skill—have been removed
one by one as objects for study, like jewels or gold antiquities
plundered from a violated tomb.

My wife stirs, bothered by the light. I put the photo back
like a body returned to its dark slot by a student
who has studied the heart's anatomy far into the night
and whose brain can retain nothing more. As he steps outside,
still weighing the phantom heft of the pericardial sac, rain
like an aromatic spirit revives his memory, and looking up
at the pulseless black vault of sky, he can only begin to imagine
how such things could ever be coaxed to beat again.

PLATO'S BREATH

The first law is the conservation law.... It says that while
energy can never be created or destroyed it can be
transformed from one form to another....We've all heard it
said that 'there's nothing new under the sun.' You can prove
it to yourself with the next breath you take. You have just
inhaled about 50 million molecules that were once inhaled
by Plato.

—Jeremy Rifkin, *Entropy: A New World View*

High above the Agora, a woman stares through intractabilities
of time and distance while her husband reads aloud
from his *Fodor's*. Her legs still burn from the long climb
up the slick marble steps to the Parthenon, her pulse a timpani
of vague omens in the white and blinding heat. Pointing to the place
where the guidebook says Socrates died, her husband recounts
the famed teacher's final hours, he who taught us all to steer
clear of the unexamined life, how he offered proofs for the eternal
life of the soul even as the quaffed poison crept toward his heart.
The woman tries to imagine such philosophic poise,
but her mind scrolls madly to the drum of her own toiling heart,
as if her accustomed picture of the world had suddenly lost
its vertical hold. Last night, on the verandah of their hotel,
unstrung by jet lag and too much ouzo, they had danced

for the first time in years, raising their arms like Zorba
and humming what they could recall of the movie's score
while mythologized constellations spun above them
and the floodlit Acropolis towered behind with all the glamour
of a Hollywood set. Later, after the wornout tape
of their sex had finally rewound and her husband slept,
she listened to the pitch of the singing city rise until
she thought her armature of glass might break. She remembered
a professor long ago in college who had asked
his students to bring a response to the Kazantzakis novel,
and when she and the others brought back nothing
but facile academic prose he had grown sad and walked out
of the room because no one had been moved simply

to come to class and dance. A month later, he was found
hanging from a lamppost somewhere off campus.

Socrates, her husband now tells her, gave his final lesson
in the absence of Plato, his favored pupil, who stayed away
stricken with a sudden fever. Breathing this same molecular sea
in which antiquity drifts like motes of spectral dust, the woman
gazes through the haze and slowly dissipating heat of Athens
to that point on the horizon where lines converge and all
things vanish. She frames it in the lens of her Nikon, focuses
on infinity, and trips the shutter, half thinking she might
trap the immensities of a moment. She closes her eyes
and rests them against the camera's box, as if to divine
what lay inside the sealed blackness, unexposed: a room,
dimly lit, a single window open to the famed light of Attica
in late afternoon. On a bed, two lovers of beauty, two bodies
riding each other away from that terrible chasm between
the many and the one, their every labored breath another rung
on the long slow climb toward a perfect deathless abstraction.

TWO

IN FRONT OF A SMALL TOWN
RADIO STATION

Last night they won a tournament
up the road. On radio they have just told
the whole town their story. In squalls
of snow these girls bounce and
dance against the cold.
One, her green team jacket
unable to conceal her belly's
swell, stares at traffic
with eyes like voided checks.
She knows the other story:
how back at the gym the boys
brash and hard as maple boles
are shooting baskets.
She knows their loose half circle,
how the balls arc and fall
through the netted hole.
How boys dream their tomorrows
green and smooth as brook water.
How they've trained to use
the world to fierce advantage
like a blind pick and roll.
How each shot as it leaves
their hands feels just right,
like a perfect movie's
only conceivable beginning.

At first we mourned Paris,
thought of the Botticellis
in Florence we would miss.
Your new clothes lay
unopened in the closet,
not needed, for it
had not yet begun to show.

It: our only point
of reference. As if lack
of gender or name somehow
kept intact the distance.
We tried to kill ambivalence
with pictures in books:
moonscapes, Bosch aliens with tails,
webbed fingers, eyes bean
white and hard.

                Easter morning
you woke bleeding. Each time
I helped you from the bed
you said you were afraid
to look, afraid of what you might see.
I told you it was only the not knowing
if we wanted it in our lives.

The next day, a whiteout:
outside, light cancelled light.
We stayed close to the barracks and
cast no shadows. Only darker shapes
betrayed themselves.

Returning, we clung to the banked sides
of the narrow plowed path,

a kind of braille for our blindness.
Flakes stung our exposed
faces like names.

MISSOURI VOICES

I sit in the attic late
with my short-wave radio
scanning the Upper Michigan
night thick as wicker
with frequencies,
picking up voices from China,
France, Spain, Malaysia,
New York, Omaha;
ballads, talk shows, prophecy.

Only once have I heard
a peep from Missouri,
a Royals game
braided with Crystal Gayle:
Quisenberry checks the...
at second and...
A long drive!
Otis going back...

Nothing since.
Not a word from Missouri.
As if it had died.
The constellations slide
toward September,
winter, another year.
Across the wide band of night
static falls
spaghetti thick.
Missouri voices—
Brett, Hawthorne, corn,
mockingbird—
like stones thrown
short of a canyon's far rim
drop in the deep silence
between.

STALKING PRAIRIE: MADISON, SOUTH DAKOTA

Pheasants burst from stubble fields
that June day the West leaned,
dead weight of wind. On your hands
and knees, you found Beardtongue,
Brome, Blue-Eyed Grass, Sage.
Here is prairie, you said,
pointing to a patch
no bigger than a pitcher's mound.
Soon it will all be gone.

It was too early for the tall grass,
obvious blooms, so you crawled
from spot to spot, excited,
explaining it all to me,
the life and history of a place.

I listened, not to you, but
to the sound of absence, the same
sound I would soon hear
in my father's hospital room
the night he died. Beneath
a raised sheet I saw his swollen
genitals. As the morphine
bore him away, the nurse,
timing breaths, studied her watch.

I listened to the sound a woman hears
when she loses her place
and has to page back through her life
to know where she left off.

The sound I heard today
seeing pumpkins at a roadside stand

this first Fall without you,
remembering the phantom pain of prairie,
knowing how absence itself
is a strongly felt presence,
how histories, vast and wordless,
contract to things: glaciers to stones,
grass seas to stems of Camphorweed.

THE KIRBY MAN
for Toby and Laura

1. Waiting for the Kirby Man

All morning she has waited
pacing from terrazzo to parquet
in her lemon chemise.
Later she rises from her bath
a Botticellian sea.
Pink, redolent of powders
she dresses for the Kirby Man.

2. The Kirby Man Arrives

At eleven, prompt, he arrives
dark and sleek as a Doberman.
Something Dionysian
flashes in his eyes.
He advances, confident
as the ducktails
the beltbuckle worn
to the side.
He moves in her vertigo
like a French waiter.
The Kirby Man.

3. The Kirby Man Gathers the Late Morning Light

Exiled all thoughts
of Hoover, Filter Queen, Rexair.
The two glide to the living room
where he gathers the late morning light
into one magician's handkerchief
until it disappears
and there is only she
and the eel-shaped voice
of the Kirby Man.

4. The Kirby Performs

A sudden glow:
the eye of the machine
fingering the dark room
like a searchlight's beam
until it finds her
wavering like Leda
between terror and a vague desire.
It makes—not noise
but music—Vivaldi
and it holds and loops
in air like a toy hummingbird.

5. The Kirby Man Talks Metaphysics

All around you life loses its skin.
Time is a molting thing.
To be free of matter
to stand clean in the empty spaces
the voids that make us free
we must sweep the scales from our eyes
vacuum our lives of debris
the body's ash which grows
until we are thick, gross
unable to breathe.
Take this spiritual machine
and rise with me to the vacant places
on delicate wings.

6. The Omnipresence of Body Ash

Hand in hand
they range about the house—
streets of Vesmannaeyjar.
The Kirby reveals
the omnipresence of body ash.
She is weary of her landscaped life

of passion siphoned off to things.
Pain jostles with desire
for salvage by the Kirby Man.

7. Moving Beyond the Body's Ashes

It is late afternoon.
The Kirby Man has come and gone.
She sits in the living room
alone, shades pulled
children and husband not yet home
the moment free
of outside disturbance.
The barbed eye holds her
like a blinded toad.
Vivaldi swells
rarefies the room.
One edge of her life
tears loose, lashing
like a ropeless sail.
She steps out of her body
a lover from a fallen slip.
Body ash drifts in the streets
like a dark snow
and neighbors dream of Florida
ignorant of their own appointments
with the Kirby Man.

THE CAT IN THE HAT: A SEQUEL

for Theodor Geisel

My children, rapt and hysterical each time
I read them the story, demand it tonight
over and over until I relent, knowing
how much at six I too would have loved
that whiskered anarchist, his magic chapeau,
the giggles triggered by his tricks,
by trouble he multiplies with such glitz
and brio, rules shattered freely as
kitchen dishes, restored on the last few
pages so Mother, happily absent, never knows.

As the children, pillowed and warm, settle
on the Big Bed, some rancorous cell squirms
in me to preface the text, to tell the rest
of the story, how sequels can come years later
when at muster each morning in the mirror
above the sink, eyes still try to believe
their fiction that nothing much has changed.

How the story's window gives out to simple rain,
how years bring new and unpredicted weathers
when there's nothing to do but sit in a house gone
suddenly strange and silent. How doors
slam, things topple and scatter for good
or ill there's no picking up. How in time
a man longs to see again his mother, young once
more, come home such long distance through the rain,
home to his rhymeless troubles right on cue
so loss and gainless pain can be recouped.

But that's not the story my children want
to hear, and though they cannot read, they're severe
with me for the slightest trace of straying.
So I say the tale anew, recite it as if

I'd been saying it all my life, much
like a true lover too pained by infidelity
not to repeat the living lie.

DEAD LANGUAGE
for Mario Puricelli, S.J.

When the priest asks for your translation
of the twenty assigned lines you feel strange
as the tangled phrases on your page
must look to him each night he stares
at your homework, every sheet, even this,
intended for the greater glory of God.
You are thirteen, new in this school, and not even
Catholic, have never heard of Jesuits or "ponies"
to ride through Latin, know nothing
about case, inverted order of words, inflections,
the three-part division of Gaul. What you want
from gender has not yet been learned
from the girl who first allows you to move
beyond monogrammed mysteries
of cashmere sweaters to the hands-on riddle
of her brassiere. Something insistent and hard rides
in your pocket and will not subside.
To this gaunt tendon of a man in black
cassock, hands smelling of soap and sacrifice,
you want to say, were it not for fear,
that your true father says it's a dead language
only fish eaters speak, and only when
they are eating God in a muddle of incense
and bells which last week left you rising
always at wrong times during Mass
for a classmate's dead mother.

It will be years before your father ceases to speak,
his tongue made tuneless by accidents
in the brain. It will be years before you leave
your wife and find yourself sitting alone
at a window puzzling over deaths

of dozens of Incan languages, or the way
the voice of Homer filled with silence,
all its heat exchanged for coldness on a page.
It will be years before it occurs to you to hope
that somewhere that very moment a new language
is being made, or that Latin is being spoken
again in shops and lovers' beds and on street
corners in casual talk of weather.

But with this priest, what you know
you know, and though you can't quite say
what dead language means, you've seen
enough. Enough at least until that moment
weeks later when you and he see what has lain
beneath your failure with words, and you know
then in a way you will only a few times ever
again in your life, once three years later
with that same girl, now sweaterless
in the back seat of your '57 Olds,
your hands parsing the living language
of her body part by part of speech
while on the radio a DJ plays songs
which some thirty years later as they return
in a resurrection of the '50's will speak
to you as only the voice of an old lover
can speak, coming as it does suddenly
over the phone far too late to be of use.
A voice like the one you imagine you will hear
on a train a few years before your death
when you are travelling through a foreign place
with strangers, listening to a language
you neither read nor speak, each word impressing
itself in the warm wax of memory,
as if you were the last monk in the world's sole
remaining scriptorium, your hand's steady movement
a mystery, divine, a small enlightened miracle.

On this Sarasota beach, varicose with old people
combing for flawless scallops and periwinkles, packed
with beautiful young women in flamboyant bikinis,
their lean tanned boyfriends close at their side, a man finds himself
thinking about desire, how Lao Tsu traced back to it
all human disappointment, how he said over and over
that the Tao written down is never the eternal
Tao, then wrote it down anyway as he rode off
into the desert to die, his heart sick
with the ways of men.
                              Once, on the heaving deck
of a boat racing across the Strait of Gibraltar,
Spain receding, Morocco reaching out to him
like a great sexual hunger, the man saw a great fish
twist free from the convoluted blue of sea,
as if in a moment something had crossed over
that he might glimpse what waited on the other side
of need. That night, in a palpably strange
room of a hotel near the Casbah he had tried to talk
about that fish, that moment, but the woman
he travelled with, intoxicated by dark
men in djellabas, by the press of peddlers
and the black beautiful eyes of begging children,
had insisted first on a version of making love peculiar
to that present and precise moment, so he wrote the fish
later into one of the many small notebooks
he carried, to be kept, or lost, or thrown
away as inertia bore him scarcely resisting
down its wide and placid stream.
                              Last night, reading
in a room far removed from that woman and the others
who had taken her place, he came upon a passage
that said the psychological present has been estimated

to lie somewhere between 2.3 and 12 seconds.
Too fragile a fulcrum, he thought, for the dead weights
of memory and anticipation. Today as the sun
assaults his pale casing of skin he knows
he can no longer take much for granted.
Red flags say this day's hidden currents make swimming
dangerous. Trapped years before in an undertow,
he will not swim. He thinks again
of that moment on the boat, of his own present
middle C of desire, surprised by the dullness
of regret. If such a fish should leap
up now from the serene blue beyond this beach,
his eyes might just as easily turn back
to satisfactions of sand at his feet, to the search
for a few undamaged shells that would make this day
end like a perfectly wrapped package,
like a small light left burning each night from the habit of fear.

APHASIA: THE BREAKDOWN OF LANGUAGE

Does a stone float on water?
the therapist asks as I watch
through one-way glass. He shrugs,
left with only the body's tentative
phrasings. By trade an accountant,
my father's lost track of numbers,
cannot match words with things:
hat with the hat, *spoon* with
the spoon this young woman displays.
I have seen the CAT scan, X-rays,
the vast shadows cast across the moon
of his brain, its eclipse leaving
a rind, a ring of brightness, prelapsarian,
for now he begins to sing a sweet hymn
as if he were Caedmon and she
his dream angel come from God
to cure his tongue of dumbness:
Jesus loves me, this I know,
For the Bible tells me so...
leaving me speechless on the short drive
home while rain stammers its refrain
on glass and gray city pavements,
hosannas of inarticulate praise.

THE WOMAN IN BLUE

I yell: *Watch this!* to my wife and children.
It's summer, we have hiked half way up the ski hill,
and with a boy's impish reflex I release
the discarded tire I have righted, instantly pleased
how it keeps its balance over bumps, gathering speed.
An instant more, and it's past retrieving. I see
beyond impulse to consequence, the way it is with words
you would sometimes take back if only you could.

Below, a road thick with traffic, the lodge windows'
great spans of glass, a house, an old woman
all in blue working her garden moments ago, but now
waving wildly up at me, or the tire, or both.
Watching that tire, I am a mix, panicked, transfixed,
the way divinity must feel, or so I want
to believe, when one of its bolts of lightning forks
eenie meenie mynie mo toward a field green and full

of Little Leaguers. Later, after the tire has bounced
harmlessly off the side of the lodge, after the woman
in blue has rebuked me for another tire that once crashed
through her living room window, exploding her TV
into flame, after a stiff drink to ease my nerves, I recall
a distant summer morning. I had taken my place
with a friend at a local dairy behind a high pile of slush
dumped by milk trucks after their morning runs. Our ammo

pile of snowballs waited for the yellow Troost trolley
to waddle slowly to its corner stop and idle
like a huge sitting duck. My friend, later to sign
for big bucks with the Cardinals and known
already across the city for his high vicious fast one,
had worked his first throw into a delicious
seamless ball of ice, which left his hand as soon
as the trolley appeared, a white streak of speed

hissing in the summer heat, no target but the mind's
home plate. I can still see the open window,
the man, someone perhaps like my father, bound
for work in town and reading, his glasses going crazy
into the air when the icy pitch connected, denial
forming on my lips even as my friend and I
scrammed up the alley. The same way it formed
with the tire, only now there is no hope of escape:

conscience, wife, children, the false frontage
of middle age. In truth, now I am more like that man
with glasses, a tireless victim of one childish sniping
or another. I know how he must have picked
up the broken spectacles, stared at the incongruity
of snow on his newspapered lap, followed their backs
as those two boys scurried madly away, his heart
diastolic with murder. I know his legs must have felt

heavy as he clambered off the trolley to chase
what he knew he had no hope of catching, anger
and fear and death all strong in his mouth
like a rancid bouillabaisse. I looked back only once
to see him stopped and out of breath beneath the silent
marquee of the local theater, his arms pumping
wildly, just like that woman in blue, that same urgent
semaphoric warning that baffles less and less.

The blinding blow spins him around in the snow
like the top in a game of skittles. Like me, like many of you,
this man has gone out of his way all his life to avoid
trouble. Oh yes, it may have found him a time or two

but he had always been nimble enough. Today he had wanted simply
to leave work early, before the paralyzed city pulled its plows
from impassable streets. At home, his wife, their lone child, a faithful,
bone-battening mutt all wait, a fat chicken even now

stewing in its own sweet juices, a nice white wine
already chilled. After lunch, her voice slightly flushed, she had called
to tell him her temperature said it was time once again.
Three straight spontaneous bleedings, and their life had stalled

as surely as the human traffic struggling homeward along
this dim and drifting boulevard. Now their summons to love
is mapped and comes from factual, calibrated measures
of heat. A second blow slows his spin, a shove,

and then he's face down and dazed in wet snow. *Wallet*?
Watch? he wonders. A groan deep in his belly tells him to rise
and strike back at this lump of shadow now poised
over him. His streetwise self says otherwise.

He sees the shoe, clownish, oversized. Ribs crack, teeth
shatter, hematomas bloom up and down his thighs. Shamed,
he rests on all fours, as if someone might be counting, blood
dripping pictographs in the trampled snow. Trained

as we are to ask, And *then* what happens? let's leave him
there, a cipher in snow–breathless, beaten, brutish, bleeding–
waiting for his graceless death. Think instead of this shadow,
its blind wants and rutting hungers. Think of what the wife needs

as she waits in the wings of her suburb, hand pressed
to her breast, her life now spinning with one simple ring
of the phone. Think of that ovulated seed, little hitchhiker waiting
for the ride that never comes. Of the dog, boneless. And should
    it bring

us this far, our unfinished story, think of the next good husband,
    ready to clutch
this broken family like a racer's baton and run the best leg
he has it within him to run. *Not enough* you shout? Your appetite
cries for something more? A bit of meaning, at least a slim peg

on which to hang this late-breaking story, a small point where
the mind might rest? Go on then. Add more snow. Let the plot thicken.
Let the story be at least the sum of its parts: meat of light, meat
of darkness. Thigh, wing, leg, breast. Think. Think of the chicken.

THREE

Speaking of contraries, see how the brook
In that white wave runs counter to itself.
It is from that in water we were from
Long, long before we were from any creature. . . .

It is this backward motion toward the source,
Against the stream, that most we see ourselves in,
The tribute of the current to the source.
It is from this in nature we are from.
It is most us.

—Robert Frost, from
"West Running Brook"

DOOR HANGING

Upstairs I have paced all day
hammering on intangibilities.
Downstairs in the kitchen
the old Finn kneels in shavings
finding a special grace
in the cough of plane on wood.
His tools circle him like toys.
Ancient hands dance
in the sweet music of grains.
This old man knows
the value of a snug fit.
The door and jamb will meet
as tightly as his beveled days.
When he leaves he says with a smile:
Today I have made a door.
What have you made?

Old man, perhaps for you
the setting sun latches into place
but do not be fooled
by the confidence of tools.
Days, private worlds
cannot be engineered like cabinets.
Hard jobs cry for
(but cannot find)
the proper hinge.
We shim ourselves
not through well-made doors
but the empty spaces they fill.
The warps and cracks
that leave our frames out of square
our lives mercifully ajar.

SPERM TEST

Here in lavatory dark you're thrown
along with this small, ludicrous cup
back on your own uninspired devices.
Here after weeks of wheat germ,
bans on heat and brief-style underpants
you labor (minus candle, music, proper
props) like blind Milton for your muse:
Liz Taylor in *Butterfield 8*, Ava
Gardner, a waitress you still remember
from an all-night diner years ago
on some irretrievable interstate.

This handiwork demands you juggle light
switch, foot to prop shut a lockless
door, your clutched specimen
cup with questions of timing, rhythm,
and whether to sit or stand.
Through thin walls you hear nurses
at their station drinking coffee,
gossiping over blind dates
and the slow progress of tomatoes.

Each countdown's marred by holds,
but you're inching toward ignition
with a dancer on *Solid Gold* (that Amerasian
with the sable rope of hair)
when someone rattles the door
and again the mission's scrubbed.
Though flintless from visions
of white-coat technicians bent
to their scopes, sifting sluggards
from swifts, normal ovals from freaks
with split tails, hydrocephalic heads,
still you try to kindle scenes
from letters to *Penthouse* magazine.

But each spark you stoke to life falters
at thoughts of what the pamphlets call
fertile man, their language lush
as delta bursting green: one meager
teaspoon for this paragon teems with more
than four hundred million perfect
spermatozoa. Like the piqued child,
you need someone, something
to blame: Your mother for urging
you conserve? A spendthrift purse
for its wild splurges on solo pleasure?
Wet dreams, foams, Trojans sneaked
from wallets and bedside tables?

But no...You collect yourself
and spell relief with Lana Turner,
and once again you stand tall,
zip, and buckle. Long ago you learned
a man's credence derives from posture.
In the hall you'll swagger slightly
for the nurses. On tile, a brash silver
tintinnabulation of sterling spurs.
Like John Wayne, your gun is legend.
Your carriage must say you know each dead end
street, each blind alley hides a stranger
truth than this your hand now tenders.

WINTER STORM

The night ice and wind left power
lines writhing in the streets
like sparkler-tongued vipers

they had gone outside to connect
his battery, dead, to hers,
bringing his car sputtering back

to life. Upstairs, in a house made dark,
ill-fitting, and cold by both children
away at college, they had made love,

sudden, unmapped, and for no reason
except their human reflex
for imitation, desire arcing back

and forth between them with the pure
voltage of long absence until it
had been sapped. When she left

for a moment, naked, her beauty
that of pale fallen petals, he tried to account
for what had been lost: a glowing iron's

heat exchanged with the cold
air around it. A child's toy, discarded,
its batteries left on, forgotten. No matter.

In time they had become the perfect measure
of what was still left but unavailable.
When she returned, they lay

spliced together again, lightly touching,
listening: to the wind's violence, to sleet
on paned glass, to blood picking its way

through thickened arteries, caution-lit
crews combing streets for limb-downed
lines, repairing what they can.

ON A CHILD'S NOSE SWALLOWED
BY A DOG

Who can blame the father? Panic
of axe blows, hunting knife probed
deep into the mutt's belly.
And who with eyes can shut them
to the moment of parting, that gulp
of human meat, cartilaginous lump
sunk deep in acidic seas, its fine
cilia undulant as tidal grasses?

For a moment, think of the nose,
which lies between *noose* and *Nostradamus*.
Those who've had pimples there
or a stray elbow already know
something of the primacy of noses,
how they lunge first into battle
and have come *pars pro toto* to stand
in their easy blood and breakage
for purely human vulnerability,
a joyous embracing of risk.

Whiskey flamed my Uncle Floyd's nose
bright enough Mother said to light candles by.
In grammar school, noses were always dead
giveaways for Jews, Father told us.
Growing up, I imagined how toward the end
Nazis must have parsed profiles
in crowds, the last tedious detail
work of problem-solving.

I've read of Indian tribes who cut
noses from adulterous women for symbol's
sake, then fashion new ones.
I myself like the broad taste women have

in noses, their fondness for odd shapes
and sizes that signify some higher
character in a man, or so they say,
though one suspects truer motive lies
in the old saw: *a long nose is a lady's*
liking. Once I dated a woman with a nose
job who described over drinks one night
how a Boston surgeon-aesthete teased
Plato from her dull quotidian dough,
beating crude plebeian gold
into airy perfection men dream of.

Not like that girl born without a face
I once read of in a magazine.
A small defect of birth left her
features fetal, unmigrated, jumbled
as a Braque or Picasso head:
nostrils for eyes, brows and lids
on cheeks, lips in the middle
of her forehead's scowl, mouth nothing
but a ragged hole for food and breath.
All found sunk in embryonic bog
and all come round and down at last
to proper slots, like parts of speech,
all but the nose, never found.

And thus she went, unbuttoned
before the world, minus that totem
we hold in air, look down, follow,
win by, wipe, tweak, pick, pay through,
brown, keep to grindstones, wind,
in or out of others' business.
That gristled meat we count, greet
our weather with, are led by or lead,
cut off for spite, cuff, make swell
with lies, jealousy, lust,
or a chronic catarrh.

In a world growing dull with sameness
imagine the infinite permutations
of skin, cartilage and bone: the juts,
snubs, and swales, fine grades
of Roman, Greek, Retroussé, the sure
cursive of septal-vestibular flare,
papillae delicate as the breast
nipples' filigree, the three turbinate
shelves sifting dusty debris, warming
breath for its pink plunge lungward.

Think of vestige physiognomy
in *schnozzle, nozzle, bugle, beezer,*
beak. Germans read the future
in a nose's itch. Others say a kiss
is on its way. For a time, Freud believed
noses were the seat of neurosis
and took suspicious shapes
from masturbation. For heart pain
and migraines, he seared
his mucous membranes with a cautery
and studied secretions rapt as Galileo
musing over falling bodies.

The nose is the seat of scent, a sense
more potent than we recognize.
Months after he died I smelled my father
smoking downstairs at first light
and I've read that ghosts often betray
themselves to us first through the nose.
So much of memory is olfaction,
the fleeting scents we link to gains
and losses: teaberry gum, lilacs, sex
of morning sheets, unbleachable odors
of lost lovers.

Who then can blame the child's father?
What joy to surface from his visceral dive,

the boy's nose raised like a prize,
as if it were the whole child himself,
fetched back to breath and light
through the hole in some farm pond's ice.
Sweet archetype! The nose came back and grew,
sewn with sutures one-third the width
of human hair, no harm, no worse for wear,
his father claims, almost like new,
almost the purest pattern of divorce
and reconciliation, a story with a moral
for a change, faintest echo of golden days
when masks came off at play's end
and every forest loss was soon mended
by a marriage or a dance.

BANKING

First class on a fluke, a case
of overbooking, and I am banking
at noon high above the Twin Cities,
San Francisco with its crab and avocado
and *dim sum* rich in my veins
like sunken chests of gold
doubloons. Entranced by new mintage

of sun on wing, the ambient sound of jet engines,
all dubieties disappear: no gravity fears,
no nightmares of Third World hungers, pampered
as I am with wine, lobster, warm damp towels
for my lemon butter hands. Against a frozen lake, random
similes of land appear, wooded umlauts, ellipses,
and ampersands. There, farther starboard,

another lake, bright against a black
circumstance of winter trees,
enough like Italy to pleasure my form-
seeking eye and recall, quietly now,
Florence, cancelled nights when spent passion
bent over a woman and me, hot, crepuscular,
like dusk over Fiesole's scalloped hills.

Slowly we bank the other way,
our turns pure, instinctual, sure
as a life mapped out only once,
long ago in perfect weather, never
in need of mid-flight corrections.
A young woman several rows up
has surprised me all morning, stealing

interested stares. Only a few
minutes of air left, I dare
to look back, she away. I want

her name for a souvenir, want
to tell her she looks like Sigourney
Weaver, but it's a line unlike
the one from which my life depends

and we've begun our scheduled descent.
Cars tear along their dotted lines
of interstate, houses, yards of snow
rise up benign to meet us. An ice-free
tarmac obtrudes nary a skip
of the heart. There's plenty of time
to waste, I know my gate, attendants tip

us with a parting gift: no delays anywhere
today. I make my final check, leaving
nothing overhead or underneath to say
Here, in this unearned, unpaid-for seat, a man
of sudden, unaccustomed riches slipped
in slick as a greased camel passing
through the needle's napping eye.

SHIT HAPPENS

There in the Citgo station, a rack of hats
my sons lock onto and laugh: the bills
sporting plastic splats of gull droppings, crowns
announcing our latest metaphysical slogan,
a mix of braggadocio and resignation:
Shit Happens. It's everywhere now,
beach towels, bumper stickers, tee-shirts.
A grassroots movement, if you will,
a slow, inexorable dawning of awareness,
not to be stopped, a vote cast for truth
in advertising, a widely shared belief
in diaper-wise philosophizing.

Contents? Nothing new.
Sophocles heard it long ago in the sound
of the Aegean, so Matthew Arnold
tells us in his own elegy to Hope,
and Camus knew it when he urged
us to imagine Sisyphus
happy. Shakespeare, too, except
the ruck of his words looks too much
like gridlock for the message
to get through. *Tell it like it is,*
we say, so we do, and when clock alarms
sound and events flock each dawn
in wave after wave of airborne
hippopotami, payloads groaning
with their wiseass bombs, we take it,
we grin, wipe clean our bald pates,
our dripping chins, and walk bravely on.

GAME OF TOUCH

It's a late summer game of touch,
two hands anywhere, third and long.
In the huddle my son, who wants to grow up
as John Elway, tells me to fake left,
then run deep to the right sideline
for his bomb. I snap the ball, stumble
and lug left all the way smack
into the zone's stacked coverage.

When I return, he says, *Dad, you're not*
paying attention! Something I accuse
him of almost every day, something I used
to say to my father as he hid
behind his drink and evening paper
and played deaf to my repeated questions.
Only after the stroke did he finally begin
to listen, cocking his head as my words came
dealt to him suitless and constantly shuffling.

I could make excuses: the madcap
interference my taped heart commits,
the gaps between real and imagined grace,
the rust and dust that penalize
my few remaining moves, the sluice
of joy a moment of perfect timing brings.
I could say that overnight one crazed
oak on the hill has set its robes aflame
like a zealous monk in an indolent
throng of green, and that's far

from being wrong, but it's something
he will not be ready to touch for years,
when he is earless to his own son's
interrogative fears. And this *is*

a game of touch, so back in the huddle
again I tell him it's last down now and still
long, no time for punts. And we dive
into our book of plays for the one
we've been saving, the one we diagram
in dust, the prayer-like heave
for boom or bust, the sleeved trick
that works once, and once only.

WALT WHITMAN AT TIMBER CREEK

after an account by Justin Kaplan

Twice the fangs struck his brain,
his left side hanging stringless for a time,
his tongue lolling like a giraffe's.
Constellations drift paralyzed, silent,
while he rides the pitch and grope of vertigo,
scrabbling for chairs, old certainties
snatched from reach by miscreant children.

By day, a taut wire thrums in his head
at the comings and goings of vague shapes.
By night, the ceaseless hiss of darkness
leaking from the room.

So he comes to Timber Creek.
Behind the thick willow curtain,
stripped naked, he wallows
in the marl pit's mud.
With a stiff brush he rubs
the grit like pumice into his skin as
he bathes in the creek's waters.

Fat, tanning, singing the name
of everything he meets
he dances his lame arabesques
to mullein blooms,
to dragonflies mated on the breeze.
Ringed by calamus, cattails,
he hears cicadas sing
of seventeen years buried
in the dark of earth
nestled to a root.
He wrestles saplings supple as boys,
feels their juices stir in him.
In the sweet grass, he dreams of Druids,

falls in love with the bodies of trees,
hears the wind's tongue
move among the branches.

It does not matter
that the hawk, stropped shadow,
circles omens in the blue
crown of sky. The constellations
spin and sing once more,
and the limp world has come firm again.

KILLER HOLD

My son, at sixteen gangly and gimped from overnight
spurts of growth, leans into the doorway, fakes,
then pumps a jumper at some imagined hoop above
his mother, who sits at the kitchen table reading the paper.
When he asks what's for supper, I look up from the stove
to where he stands, all feet, the crazed geometry
of adolescence in all its pending beauty of bony lines
and angles, and I offer him a taste of the cold beer
I have just opened. His face records its usual disgust.
The last few years have pared away much of his sense
of my humor. Nevertheless I give him a playful little shove.
Come on, I say, putting aside my wooden spoon.
Today's the day, I can feel it, I tell him,
and I throw a jab or two at that handsome face
trapped between a man's and a boy's.
He bobs and weaves as I softly slap at his stubble chin
so impossibly in need of a shave and try to sucker him in.
This routine has become a standing joke. I want him
now, I tell him, before I lose my thinning advantage.
À la an aging Muhammad Ali, I float, I rope-a-dope,
while his reptile brain contends with commonsense
to calculate the relative gains and losses. *Nope*,
he says in his newly adopted monosyllabic mode.
As he grins, I strike, and too late he tries to twist away
from the choke hold I planned while he was cerebrating.
Left to its own devices, my Bolognese sauce has reached
a slow molten volcanic roll, bubbling and spotting
the white surface of the stove like a steady spatter
of blood. My pan of fettuccine is close to screaming
al dente. Any moment, the garlic bread will burn
to a blackness beyond redemption. The salad, dressed,
waits. The wine, its breathing labored, is ready
to be poured. Beneath my left arm crooked about his throat,

I feel the mastoid sheath flexed taut like the skin of a drum
about to be struck. Within, I picture his twin
carotid arteries, the fragile cairn of vertebral bone,
each bellowed breath punching its way up the dark
shaft from his beleaguered lungs. His mother, growing
less and less amused, puts down the news and pleads
for his release from this, my killer hold. With my free hand
I reach behind me to turn down the heat beneath the sauce
and pasta. In his arched resistance, I feel the faintest
promise of defeat. I am not yet ready to let go.

THE CATCH

Baby Hurtles from Tenement Window;
Ex-Tight End Makes Save

        —newspaper headline

They say the Lord's eye sees
every precious thing, and she
was that, even to a father blind with rage who
stripped her from her mother's grasp
and, four floors up, threw
her through the curtained window's glass.

Something dark and ravening flew
with that child into the first flute
of Brooklyn's morning light. Fear
said: *Cover your eyes!* to a man
looking up from the cankered street. *Here,*
as always, said his rough instinctual hands.

Blank, absent, he made the catch
of a lifetime. Sweet Jesus. Oh match
struck at random in this catacombed night!
Children still are falling, falling fast
and something takes with black delight
our marbled hearts for its repast.

Fated Savior, sate with gall this appetite.
Fix us with your stony eye.
Catch us with your bony arms at last.

My special gratitude to the following, whose poems, instruction, and encouragement have sustained me in the long making of this book: Donald Junkins, Laurie Kutchins, Carole Oles, William Trowbridge, and Stephen Dobyns.

Thanks are due to the editors of the following periodicals in whose pages these poems, sometimes in slightly different versions, first appeared: "Saved" in *The Atlanta Review*; "The Kirby Man" and "Thoughts On A Child's Nose Swallowed By A Dog" in *The Laurel Review*; "Antediluvian: Kansas City, Summer, 1953" in *The Nebraska Review*; "First Fantasy," "Spring Burial," and "Stopping to Dance" in *New Letters*; "Door Hanging" in *Passages North*; "Aphasia: The Breakdown of Language" in *Poet & Critic*; "In Front of a Small Town Radio Station" in *Tendril*; "Thirty-Fifth Bombing Mission, Cerignola, Italy" and "Stalking Prairie: Madison, South Dakota" in *Interim*; "Missouri Voices" in *The Chariton Review*; "Dead Language" in *Zone 3*; "The Psychological Present" in *The Centennial Review*; "The Cat in the Hat: A Reprise" in *Nightsun*; "Banking" in *The MacGuffin*; "Shit Happens" in *Tar River Poetry*; "Winter Storm" in *The Cream City Review*; "Walt Whitman at Timber Creek" in *The Mickle Street Review*; "Supply, Demand" in *Green Mountains Review*; "Hints for Dissection: Gray's Anatomy* in *The Marlboro Review*.

A number of the poems in this book were also published in two chapbooks, *Running Patterns* (Flume Press, 1985) and *Hand Shadows* (GreenTower Press, 1988).

Poems in this collection have also been included in the following anthologies: "Door Hanging" in *The 1984 Anthology of Magazine Verse & Yearbook of American Poetry* (Monitor Books) and in *The Passages North Anthology* (Milkweed Editions, 1990); "Missouri Voices" in *The 1985 Anthology of Magazine Verse & Yearbook of American Poetry* (Monitor Books); "In Front of A Small Town Radio Station" in *Inheriting the Land: Contemporary Voices from the Midwest* (The University of Minnesota Press, 1993).

Randall R. Freisinger's poems have appeared in *Tendril, New Letters, The Laurel Review, The Chariton Review, Passages North, Interim, The Milkweed Chronicle, The Nebraska Review, Poet & Critic, Zone 3, The Cream City Review, Tar River Poetry, The Atlanta Review, Green Mountains Review, The North Coast Review, The Marlboro Review,* and many other literary magazines.

Nominated four times for the Pushcart Prize, his work has been included in the 1984, 1985, and 1997 editions of *Anthology of Magazine Verse & Yearbook of American Poetry* (Monitor Books), in the *Passages North Anthology* (Milkweed Editions, 1990), and in *Inheriting the Land: Contemporary Voices from the Midwest* (University of Minnesota Press, 1993).

Freisinger has published two chapbooks. *Running Patterns* won the 1985 Flume Press National Chapbook Competition (David Wojahn, judge). *Hand Shadows* was published in 1988 by Green Tower Press (editor, William Trowbridge). *Plato's Breath* is his first book-length collection.

Born and raised in Kansas City, Missouri, he was educated at the University of Missouri–Columbia. Since 1977, he has lived in Michigan's Upper Peninsula, where he is Professor of Rhetoric, Literature and Creative Writing in the Department of Humanities at Michigan Technological University. He serves as Associate Editor for *The Laurel Review.*

The May Swenson Poetry Award was named for May Swenson, and honors her as one of America's most provocative, insouciant, and vital poets. During her long career, Swenson published eleven volumes of poems, and she was loved and praised by writers from virtually every major school of poetry. She left a legacy of nearly fifty years of writing when she died in 1989.

May Swenson lived most of her life in New York city, the center of poetry writing and publishing in her day. But she is buried in Logan, Utah, her hometown.